Prentice Hall's

STUDENT REFLECTION JOURNAL

FOR STUDENT SUCCESS

Susan Landgraf

PEARSON

Prentice Hall

Upper Saddle River, New Jersey
Columbus, Ohio

Pearson Prentice Hall™ is a trademark of Pearson Education, Inc.
Pearson® is a registered trademark of Pearson plc
Prentice Hall® is a registered trademark of Pearson Education, Inc.

12 13 14 15

ISBN 0-13-113130-3

Table of Contents

Preface

Journaling or keeping self-reflective notes doesn't mean we write succinctly and clearly. Rather journaling is a work in progress, a means to become aware of our thoughts and feelings so we can think about them further.

In addition, words in a journal allow us the luxury of going back. We have a trail we can follow to see where we've come from. More often than not, that journal also shows where we'd like to go – new territory both in terms of our emotions and our actions.

Think of this journaling book as a means to "get what you want" from yourself and from your life. You can even see it as an "icon" in the way Thomas Moore describes: "Our notebooks…truly become our own private gospels and sutras, our holy books, and…truly serve as icons, every bit as significant in the work of our own soul as the wonderful icons of the Eastern churches are for their congregations."

This journal is intended to help you map your life now – and in the future.

Enjoy discovery.

Susan Landgraf

Section 1: Purpose

Why are you in college?

Some Information

- Purpose, according to *Webster's New Collegiate Dictionary*, is synonymous with "intention," "by intent," "on purpose."
- "The purpose of life is a life of purpose," Robert Byrne said.
  "First say to yourself what you would be; and then do what you have to do."
  Epictetus

_____

_____

_____

_____

_____

_____

_____

_____

_____

_____

_____

_____

_____

_____

Ideas to write about

What do you want in life? Why did you decide to go to college? How is being in college helping you find or fulfill your purpose.

_____

_____

_____

_____

_____

_____

_____

_____

_____

_____

_____

_____

_____

_____

_____

_____

_____

_____

Beyond the Classroom

Make two lists. In the first, list what you are getting out of your college education now. In the second, list what your college education will mean in the future.

Example:

Now	After graduation
Credits	Use your degree as a "credibility builder" on your resume
Communication skills	Communicate more effectively with your fellow employees, customers, boss
Speech class	Give successful business presentations
Service learning projects	Use as a "credibility builder" on your resume

_____

_____

_____

_____

_____

_____

_____

_____

_____

_____

_____

_____

Section 2: Academic Expectations

Do you know what's expected?

Some Information

You're in college now, not grade 13.

- Your rights include, among others:

    Freedom to inquire
    Pursuit of your educational objectives
    Use of college programs and resources appropriate to your course of study

- In return, you are expected to:

    Follow state laws and college policies
    Learn and analyze information
    Turn in college-level work

_____

_____

_____

_____

_____

_____

_____

_____

_____

_____

Ideas to write about

What do the words "rights" and "expectations" mean to you?

_____

_____

_____

_____

_____

_____

_____

_____

_____

_____

_____

_____

_____

_____

_____

Beyond the Classroom

Does your college have a booklet that spells out students' rights and responsibilities? How are these policies, rights, and responsibilities similar to policies, rights, and responsibilities in the work place? For instance, colleges list plagiarism as grounds for being expelled. Companies list stealing as grounds for being fired.

_____

_____

_____

_____

_____

_____

_____

_____

_____

_____

_____

_____

_____

_____

_____

_____

_____

_____

Section 2: Academic Responsibilities

Some Information

In higher education you're being asked not only to think but to "think actively." This means:

- Take responsibility for your actions and your education

- Attend classes and be an active participant

- Learn independently outside of class

- Work with others

- Put into practice what you know – on tests, reports, projects or presentations per the criteria spelled out in each class

_____

_____

_____

_____

_____

_____

_____

_____

_____

_____

_____

_____

Ideas to write about

Do you find being in college easier than you imagined or more difficult? Is this because
you are being held accountable at the same time you have more freedom?

_____

_____

_____

_____

_____

_____

_____

_____

_____

_____

_____

_____

_____

_____

_____

_____

_____

_____

Beyond the Classroom

Talk to an advisor or an educational planner regarding your courses and academic program. Take notes.

Or compare this time in your life to when you first started school -- new surroundings, new "authority" figures," new things to learn and memorize. Do you think there will be similarities when you step into the work world? What might they be?

_____

_____

_____

_____

_____

_____

_____

_____

_____

_____

_____

_____

_____

_____

Section 2: Juggling Academic Expectations and Responsibilities with the Rest of Your Life

Some Information

- We've heard the advice: Live each day in the moment.

  Yet we anticipate tomorrow.

- We've heard: A journey of a thousand miles begins with a single step.

  Yet to start that journey we must set a goal and plan – not just walk back and forth each day.

  Sometimes we feel like the rabbit in *Alice In Wonderland*:
  > "I'm late, I'm late, for a very important date!
  > No time to say hello, goodbye!
  > I'm late, I'm late, I'm late!"

  Yet, we must organize and prioritize with regard to our future. Stephen Minot, professor of creative writing at the University of California, Riverside, wrote "A Final Note" in his text *Three Genres*. He was speaking to "serious" writers about writing, but his note speaks to anyone who has a passion, a plan, or an idea of what he/she wants.

  Minot wrote: "If you are in college, it will seem as if you have no time to do anything but complete your assignments. And if you are out of college, it may seem that you are being swept along with the demands of daily life. We all like to believe that we 'have no choice.' But the fact is that the allocation of time is fundamentally a matter of personal choice. Consciously or unconsciously we set priorities."

_____

_____

_____

_____

_____

Ideas to write about

What do you want to be? What do you want in your life? Do you have an image of what you'd like your future to look like? Do you find setting priorities to be difficult?

_____

_____

_____

_____

_____

_____

_____

_____

_____

_____

_____

_____

_____

_____

_____

_____

_____

Beyond the Classroom

Put **college** on one side of the page. Estimate the number of hours you're spending in college or on college-related assignments, study, etc. On the other side of the page, list the **other commitments or roles** you have outside of college.

College	Other Commitments, Roles
Attend class	Soccer
Drive to and from campus 4 hours a week	Girlfriend
Go to study group for biology	Job
Study	Pizza with buddies on Fridays

Now prioritize your list. What will matter most two years from now?

_____

_____

_____

_____

_____

_____

_____

_____

_____

_____

_____

Section 3: Critical Thinking

Is thinking hard?

Some Information

According to John Chaffee and Richard Paul, critical thinking is a process that is:
- active
- directed toward a purpose
- organized

According to Michael Scriven and Richard Paul, "Critical thinking is the intellectually disciplined process of actively and skillfully conceptualizing, applying, analyzing, synthesizing, and/or evaluating information gathered from, or generated by, observation, experience, reflection, reasoning, or communication, as a guide to belief and action.

Critical thinking requires logic and includes, therefore, reasoning.

Elements of critical thinking usually include:
- studying evidence, reasons, data, and other information
- constructing and evaluating arguments
- recognizing assumptions
- applying knowledge to new situations
- looking at other points of view and positions
- considering solutions, conclusions
- considering consequences and implications
- recognizing assumptions
- searching for additional evidence, reasons, data, and information
- being complete and fair
- being clear, accurate and precise

_____

_____

_____

_____

_____

_____

Ideas to write about

Some people say that thinking critically is "hard." Do you agree or disagree?

_____

_____

_____

_____

_____

_____

_____

_____

_____

_____

_____

_____

_____

_____

_____

Beyond the Classroom

Try this exercise:

1. Decide on a problem, dilemma, or situation you'd like to solve, resolve, or gain some insight into.

2. Then: 1. Write a brief summary (3-4 sentences; no facts)
   2. State the central problem
   3. List the key facts
   4. Give the assumptions
   5. Come up with options
   6. Make a decision
   7. Support that decision

How can you use this exercise for any problem, dilemma, or situation in your life – in college, in your personal life, in the work place?

_____

_____

_____

_____

_____

_____

_____

_____

_____

_____

_____

Section 4: Diversity

Do you like red M&Ms or yellow?

Some Information

- The demographics of our country, our communities, and our schools are changing. We in America are the world – so many cultures coming together on common ground. But "one size doesn't fit all," and key international issues challenge us – both how we work together at home with people of other cultures and with people and countries around the world.

- A report titled "Diversity Works: The Emerging Picture of How Students Benefit" by Daryl G. Smith analyzes emerging research on the effects of campus diversity on students. In a nutshell, commitment to diversity at a college is "...related to positive educational outcomes for all students, individual satisfaction, and a commitment to improving racial understanding."

- Whether you're flipping burgers and selling them to customers at the drive-in or manufacturing and selling 747s, you must work with other people.

_____

_____

_____

_____

_____

_____

_____

_____

_____

Ideas to write about

What do M&Ms have to do with diversity?

_____

_____

_____

_____

_____

_____

_____

_____

_____

_____

_____

_____

_____

_____

_____

_____

_____

_____

_____

Beyond the Classroom

What do you know about people of different nationalities, races, ethnicities? How can knowing more about other people be translated into increased productivity and job satisfaction?

_____

_____

_____

_____

_____

_____

_____

_____

_____

_____

_____

_____

_____

_____

_____

_____

_____

_____

_____

Section 5: College and Community Resources

What do you need to be successful?

Some Information

Quick references for college resources:

- Quarter or semester class schedule listing departments, classes, and other basic information
- College newspaper
- Web site
- Library

Quick references for community resources:

- Telephone service and government pages
- Local newspaper
- Library
- Search engines, such as Google, and web sites
- Community organizations such as the YMCA

_____

_____

_____

_____

_____

_____

_____

_____

Ideas to write about

Do you feel comfortable asking for help or assistance? What has been your experience in the past?

_____

_____

_____

_____

_____

_____

_____

_____

_____

_____

_____

_____

_____

_____

_____

_____

_____

Beyond the Classroom

A friend once said, "Being successful means knowing who to ask for what." Reporters, researchers, managers all have "tick" files, rolodexes, or computer files of people, organizations, etc. that might provide information.

Start a personal database, either in a computer file or in a notebook, of "resources" that might be beneficial in our academic career. Think ahead to the work world and add names and resources that might be useful in your job career.

Add to your database throughout your professional career.

_____

_____

_____

_____

_____

_____

_____

_____

_____

_____

_____

_____

_____

Section 5: Service Learning

Some Information

- Thomas Merton wrote: "No man is an island."

- The concept of service-learning combines academic studies with volunteerism. Service learning is based on the idea that learning can happen in projects that involve students in the community where they "give" something to others in the course of their learning.

- According to the National Service Learning Clearinghouse, service learning affords students the structured opportunity to accomplish tasks that link to self-reflection, self-discovery, and the acquisition and comprehension of values, skills, and knowledge.

- Service learning means that critical thinking and hands-on learning come together for the benefit of the student, the campus, and the community.

_____

_____

_____

_____

_____

_____

_____

_____

_____

_____

_____

Ideas to write about

"Service is the rent we pay to be living. It is the very purpose of life and not something you do in your spare time."

What is your response to Maria Wright Edelman's quote?

_____

_____

_____

_____

_____

_____

_____

_____

_____

_____

_____

_____

_____

_____

_____

_____

_____

_____

Beyond the Classroom

Are you interested in combining academics with volunteer work – earning credits for giving service to an organization or group? How could you use that kind of learning experience as a "credibility builder" on your resume and to "sell" yourself to an employer or company after you graduate?

_____

_____

_____

_____

_____

_____

_____

_____

_____

_____

_____

_____

_____

_____

_____

_____

Section 6: Learning Styles

How do you learn?

Some Information

There are many ways of learning. A "learning style" is a neatly packaged and labeled
way of how people process information. You may fall into one category predominately
or in all of them. But knowing how you learn – take in and process information – can
help you see your strengths and adopt strategies for overcoming learning challenges in
your academic career.

- **Auditory**: learns best through verbal instruction

Talks a lot	Likes the telephone
Talks to him/herself	Gives verbal excuses
Asks questions	Is easily distracted by sounds
Shows emotion verbally	

- **Visual**: learns best when seeing and watching

Notices details	Likes tidiness
Is distracted by visual disorder	Asks for written directions
Becomes impatient with extensive listening	Remembers faces
Shows emotion with facial expressions	Doodles, does puzzles, takes notes

- **Kinesthetic**: learns best by being "hands-on"

Touches things	Likes sports and physical activity
Remembers best what was done	Is impetuous and impulsive
Talks with active verbs and with hands	Shows emotion with body reactions
Likes to take things apart and put them back together	

- **Adaptive**: learns best by combining or using all of the above, depending on the situation
  or activity

_____

_____

_____

_____

Ideas to write about

What learning style are you? How do you learn best?

What might you do to listen more attentively; be more observant; and do more "hands-on" learning?

_____

_____

_____

_____

_____

_____

_____

_____

_____

_____

_____

_____

_____

_____

_____

_____

_____

Beyond the Classroom

How could you adapt to different teaching and management styles?

If a professor lectures, and you are a visual learner, you might try drawing pictures or making charts or graphs during the lecture (or immediately after).

If a manager or boss "tells" you what to do and you're a visual learner, what strategies could you use in the work place?

_____

_____

_____

_____

_____

_____

_____

_____

_____

_____

_____

_____

_____

_____

Section 6: Action Styles

Some Information

People also take different approaches to how they do things. You may be mostly one of the following four action style types – or a mix-and-match type.

- **Analytical/Logical**

  Likes ideas and concepts   Thinks through ideas, logical
  Prefers facts, theories and formal lectures Is critical and authoritarian
  Likes scientific and financial areas   Has goals
  Looks at the bottom line

- **Organized/Safekeeper**

  Likes control   Takes preventative action
  Prefers data, processes and structure   Is articulate and detailed
  Likes administrative and supervisory areas   Likes to be organized
  Gets things done

- **Intuitive/Feeling**

  Likes team work and goals   Listens and is supportive
  Prefers symbols, music and language   Is intuitive and expressive
  Likes teaching, training and writing areas   Touches a lot
  Reflects and works for harmony

- **Imaginative/Experimental**

  Likes to synthesize and integrate   Takes risks and speculates
  Prefers possibilities and experimentation   Is imaginative, artistic and visual
  Likes generating ideas and causing change   Breaks rules and acts impetuously
  Thrives on challenge

_____

_____

_____

_____

Ideas to write about

How do you do things? Do you fall into one category or several?

_____

_____

_____

_____

_____

_____

_____

_____

_____

_____

_____

_____

_____

_____

_____

_____

_____

_____

Beyond the Classroom

According to *The Wisdom of Teams,* "A team is a small number of people with complementary skills (and thinking modes) who are committed to a common purpose, performance goals, and approach for which they hold themselves mutually accountable."

Supposedly the most effective team is one where you have all four "action styles" represented. Though that might mean more time and effort, as people work to understand their purpose, goals and approaches, the end result likely will be more successful.

What kinds of adaptations could be made when working with people who have a different action style than you?

* If you have a manager or boss who likes control and micromanages your every move and you are an experimental type, how will you adapt to your boss' style? Will you try to become a "safekeeper" to match his or her style? Will you talk to your boss to find a compromise?

_____

_____

_____

_____

_____

_____

_____

_____

_____

_____

Section 7: Study Tips

How can you make the most of your studying and research time?

Some Information

- Write down assignments.

- The more you can break assignments and projects into "bite-size" pieces the better.

- Make an outline or draw a map of your study plan.

- Use a checklist for assignments and projects; check off each "piece" of the assignment you finish.

- Study with other students and ask each other questions.

- The more you can interact with the material you're studying the better. Take notes. Highlight or underline. Make up self-quizzes.

- Set study times – a start time and an end time. Set a timer if you like. Make the study times "bite-size" as well. Research has shown that studying in blocks of 45 minutes to an hour works better than long hours without a break. After an hour and a half or two, your ability to concentrate decreases rapidly. Take a break and/or switch to another subject.

- Know how you study best. Some people need to sit in a straight-backed chair with everything tidy on a bare desktop. Other people like to sprawl on the floor and snack while the television blares in the corner. Others like to listen to classical music or go to a coffee shop.

- Reward yourself after you study.

_____

_____

_____

_____

Ideas to write about

What is your attitude about studying? Is studying like pulling teeth for you? How can you apply some of the above tips and make studying less onerous or frustrating?

_____

_____

_____

_____

_____

_____

_____

_____

_____

_____

_____

_____

_____

_____

_____

_____

Beyond the Classroom

How would any of the tips above be helpful in any job you have now or will have in the future?

_____

_____

_____

_____

_____

_____

_____

_____

_____

_____

_____

_____

_____

_____

_____

_____

_____

Section 7: Note-Taking Guides

Some Information

- The main point in taking notes is to condense, to put the most important information down so you can refer back to it readily.

- Here are some suggestions. Not all of them work for everyone. The point is that each of us works/studies differently. But several of these might help you study better and help you retain more of what you study. You are trying to connect new information with information or experience you already know.

  - Scan the text book material and read the information at least once before lecture

  - You won't be able to write down every word, so listen for key phrases.

  - Take notes on a sheet of paper that has an inch or two-inch margin on the left. Don't write in that space until you've finished taking notes. Review your notes and write key terms (further condensing your material) in that space.

  - Use abbreviations. If you're writing about your college, write a capital "C" instead of spelling the name out each time, for example.

  - Use bullets, checkmarks, or stars to indicate key terms or information, so that when you review that information will stand out more.

  - Draw pictures or symbols in your notes, especially if you're a visual learner.

  - As soon as possible after the lecture or your own reading, word process the information or write it on 3 x 5 cards. Use them as flash cards.

  - Write up the notes in story form, as if you're telling a "story" to someone else.

_____

_____

_____

Ideas to write about

What helps you remember what you write?
Try one of the hints about how to take notes more effectively. Then free write about how
that experience worked. Did you feel self-conscious?

_____

_____

_____

_____

_____

_____

_____

_____

_____

_____

_____

_____

_____

_____

Beyond the Classroom

Taking good notes on material you hear or read helps you remember in two ways:

One, in the process of writing, you impress your mind more with the information than if you'd just listened. It's like pressing ink more deeply into paper.

Two, you have material in condensed form to refer back to.

Imagine having an informational interview with an employer? Why would good note-taking skills be important in such an interview?

_____

_____

_____

_____

_____

_____

_____

_____

_____

_____

_____

_____

_____

_____

Section 7: Test-Taking Strategies

Some Information

Prior to any test:

- Studying in small blocks of time – 45 minutes to an hour; then take a short break. Or even study in 10- and 15-minute blocks of time using the 3x5 flashcards you made from your notes.

- If you have test-taking anxiety, see someone in Counseling or Student Services.

- Don't cream for a test the night before but do eat something "sustaining," such as a bagel or oatmeal – not candy. The energy from candy dissipates quickly.

- Take two pens or pencils – or a scantron – whatever's required for the test. Be prepared.

During the test:

- Read the entire test over before you start to answer the questions. Scanning gives you time to settle in and calm your nervousness. Secondly, your mind will start warming up to key words or phrases.

- Answer the questions in the order you know them. If you don't have a "certain" answer until question #17 in a 20-question test, fine; answer question #17 and move on. Sometimes one question and its answer will give you a clue to another question. Work forward – but not necessarily in numerical order.

After the test:

- Don't beat yourself up if you didn't do well. Find out how to be more successful the next time.

- If you did well, use the same approach for the next test.

_____

_____

_____

Ideas to write about

Do you like taking tests? Do you feel anxious before a test? Most people do. Tests
mean "being tested," after all. How can you cut test anxiety – use it as a motivational
tool?

_____

_____

_____

_____

_____

_____

_____

_____

_____

_____

_____

_____

_____

_____

_____

_____

_____

Beyond the Classroom

What is a test? The *Webster's New Collegiate Dictionary* gives this definition: "a critical examination, observation, or evaluation"
and
"something (as a series of questions or exercises) for measuring the skill, knowledge, intelligence, capacities, or aptitudes of an individual or group"

How will you be "tested" in the work world?

_____

_____

_____

_____

_____

_____

_____

_____

_____

_____

_____

_____

_____

_____

Section 7: Library Research Strategies

Some Information

- The formal name for finding information is called research, and the process usually requires us to ask one or more people for information or to use sources to find that information. We read books, articles, newspapers; we look at videos and movies; we search out graphs and facts.

- Some information that exists in the world is so common we consider it part of the "common domain." This means that it belongs to "the people" and we don't have to credit a source. Examples would include: Don't touch a hot stove or you'll get burned. Namibia gained its independence in 1990.

- But when we give information written or spoken by other people in a specific context, we must give proper credit to that person. We must cite our source. If we take information that is not ours -- something someone else wrote or said – and don't credit the source, we are committing plagiarism, a serious offense that is cause for expulsion in some colleges.

  - Talk to a librarian. Ask questions. They are experts on what can be found in the library.

  - Keep a 3 x 5 card or a list of each resource. Write down the name of the publication or tape, the author(s), the title, the date published or produced, the name of the publisher, and the page numbers or the section on the tape where you found the information.

  - Copy information accurately.

  - Write numbers in numerals (10) as well as in words (ten).

  - Keep your information organized by subject or source.

  - Think about how each source or information from that source will fit into your project (proposal, paper, etc.).

  - Double-check your notes for accuracy after you've finished your project.

_____

_____

_____

Ideas to write about

What are your earliest memories of a library? Do you feel comfortable using the library or out of place, as if there's too much and you don't know where to look? Do you feel overwhelmed by research? What could you do to minimize the feeling of being overwhelmed? Start by talking to a librarian (and put your note-taking skills to work).

_____

_____

_____

_____

_____

_____

_____

_____

_____

_____

_____

_____

_____

_____

_____

_____

_____

_____

Beyond the Classroom

Most of us know a lot – from watching others, from reading, and from experience. But almost all of our lives we need to "conduct research," even if it's for something simple like deciding which car to buy. Make a list of other situations – in your life or a job you've had – where you needed to conduct research, no matter how informal that situation was. What is the common process in any type of research?

Section 7: Computer Literacy

Some Information

The World-Wide Web has opened up the world, literally, to anyone who has access to a computer. But just because the web gives us entrée to almost anything does not mean we are any more "literate" or well informed.

There are three components to being computer literate.
- One: Know how to use the computer – word process, email, conduct research through the web.
- Two: Know who has put the information out and how to judge the validity of that information.
- Three: Understand the impact of technology. According to Michael B. Eisenberg and Doug Johnson in the article "Learning and Teaching Information Technology Computer Skills in Context," one technology literacy competency that might be relevant is "having knowledge of the impact of technology on careers, society, and culture."

Remember to question what you find on the web:

- Who put out the information? Are they part of a corporation or group? Profit-making? Non-profit?
- Why would you trust the author or authors? How do they know what they know? Does their field of study warrant their supposed "expertise"?
- Why is the author or the group making the information public? What motives might he/she or they have?
- Has the author(s) cited the information? Is there a bibliography? Have you checked with the original sources to see if the quotations and information are accurate?
- What is the quality of the writing and graphics, etc.? Would you want this

  individual writing your reports or presenting your data in your stead?

- Have you tried to find at least two other sources giving the same information?

_____

_____

_____

Ideas to write about

What has been your experience with computers?

_____

_____

_____

_____

_____

_____

_____

_____

_____

_____

_____

_____

_____

_____

_____

_____

_____

_____

Beyond the Classroom

There's an old adage: Nothing is free. Some say that computers haven't saved people time; rather they use up more time. Some say that having so much information at our fingertips makes us more pessimistic.

You undoubtedly are required to use computers in your classes now and probably will have to be "computer literate" in whatever job you do. Make a list of computer practices you can think of that will make the computer a time saver rather than a waster now and on the job.

_____

_____

_____

_____

_____

_____

_____

_____

_____

_____

_____

_____

_____

_____

_____

Section 7: Listening Tips

Some Information

- Unless you're mentally ambidextrous, listen and/or do one thing at a time.

- Pay attention.

- Look at the person you're talking with or listening to.

- If the person speaks softly or you have trouble hearing, ask him/her to speak up.

- Ask questions, especially when something seems unclear. If it isn't appropriate while the person is talking, jot a note to yourself to ask him/her or a librarian or other source later.

- Read the text and gather together any previous knowledge on the topic prior to a lecture or talk.

- Make notes during a lecture or talk.

- Don't talk while someone else is talking.

_____

_____

_____

_____

_____

_____

_____

_____

_____

Ideas to write about

What kind of learner are you? Do you like listening to other people? What is it that can
catch your attention when other people are talking?

_____

_____

_____

_____

_____

_____

_____

_____

_____

_____

_____

_____

_____

_____

_____

_____

_____

Beyond the Classroom

Would you want your boss or supervisor to be a good listener? Why?

If you have trouble "listening" to others and remembering what they say, what steps could you take to "strengthen your listening habits"?

_____

_____

_____

_____

_____

_____

_____

_____

_____

_____

_____

_____

_____

_____

_____

_____

_____

Section 7: Memory-Enhancing Tips

Some Information

- The more you can engage in the accumulation of information, the more you will remember.

    o Visualize information; picture the way things look. Draw pictures.

    o Write things down. Buy or make up a calendar/scheduler where you can write due dates and "to dos." Check it daily.

    o Use verbal mnemonic devices. Saying "there is a rat" in the word "separate" may sound nonsensical; but come up with your own for words and try it. Take, for instance, the word aligned: "There is a snag in the line" for aligned.

    o Use acronyms or put words to a rhythm. Write information in rhyme.

    o Ask questions. Write down answers and then rephrase in your own words.

- Know which hours are your "peak" hours, the time when you have the best attention span and are most productive. Study or do anything that requires critical thinking then. You'll remember more.

- Eat a balanced died. Get enough sleep.

- Know why it is important for you to remember the information.

- And -- pay attention. When someone talks to you, listen. Look at them. Be fully present. When you're pumping gas, pump gas; be fully attentive. When you're memorizing information, "put mind in gear and engage fully."

_____

_____

_____

_____

_____

Ideas to write about

Do you have a good memory? Why or why not? Do you wish you could remember more? Why?

_____

_____

_____

_____

_____

_____

_____

_____

_____

_____

_____

_____

_____

_____

_____

_____

_____

_____

Beyond the Classroom

The next time you need to remember something, try one of the previous suggestions. Try several suggestions. Which ones work for you – no matter what it is you're trying to remember?

_____

_____

_____

_____

_____

_____

_____

_____

_____

_____

_____

_____

_____

_____

_____

_____

Section 8: Time Management

How would you rate your time management skills?

Some Information

Picture a basketball court without lines and hoops. A performing hall without a stage and chairs for the audience. A life without goals and plans.

Try some of these time-management tips:

- Buy an organizer or planner. Use it.

- Estimate how long a job or project will take. Start with the due date and work backwards to the present time.

- Give yourself rewards for meeting deadlines.

- Organize your life. Throw out clutter.

- Ditch expectations of yourself and others that are unrealistic.

- Ride an exercise bike and read *Moby Dick* at the same time. (You'll use up more calories that way.)

- Carry a book, magazine, or class notes with you wherever you go.

- Keep your gas tank at least half full. Make a duplicate of all your keys. Always carry two pens.

- Pause before saying "yes" to anything.

- Eat out with friends and do stretch exercises while talking on the phone.

- Team up with friends to study. Study groups mean you're likely to learn more.

- Twenty minutes of meditation is as good as an hour's nap.

- While you're doing something, be involved and concentrated on the person or task at that moment.

- Get as much sleep as you need. The average ranges from 7 to 9 hours.

Ideas to write about

Do you think that managing your time means cutting out spontaneity? Do you think that
being organized means you lead a boring life? Is there such a thing as "wasted time"?
When have you "spent" time you wish you hadn't?

_____

_____

_____

_____

_____

_____

_____

_____

_____

_____

_____

_____

_____

_____

_____

_____

_____

Beyond the Classroom

Make a list of the essentials in your life. Your list would include sleep, food, and personal hygiene. In addition, you probably will include school, studying, working, entertainment, exercise, driving and/or commuting time, friends, etc.

Prioritize your list. Sleep, food, and personal hygiene will likely all rate "No. 1"s. What comes in second and third? What likely will be most important two years from now? How will the ability to prioritize and plan help you now? In the work place?

_____

_____

_____

_____

_____

_____

_____

_____

_____

_____

_____

_____

_____

_____

Section 9: Money Management

Do you have enough money?

Some Information

$. It makes the world go round.

$. One of the biggest time and worry eaters – making it, spending it, budgeting it, working a second job for it, splurging….

$. There's a price for everything.

Try some of these money-management tips:

- Buy fewer snacks and packaged food.

- Shop thrift shops for clothing and household items.

- Take public transportation or carpool.

- Spend cash. Don't charge.

- Give yourself an allowance.

- Eat dinner before going to a movie (a matinee). Skip the popcorn and drink.

- Put your dreams into pictures. Cut them out of magazines and make collage. Keep those dreams in mind when you go shopping.

- Open at least one savings account. Designate what that money will be spent on.

- Organize your bills and financial records.

- Visualize money – the feel of it, the power of it, the negative energy of it.

- Save your change – coins and even $1 bills.

- Share books with friends. Become friendly with the local library.

- Know what things cost, how much money you save if you buy now, how much money you'll save if you don't need the item or items at all.

Ideas to write about

Most people say they never have enough money. Is that true for you? What do you wish
you had more money for? What pattern does your spending take?

_____

_____

_____

_____

_____

_____

_____

_____

_____

_____

_____

_____

_____

_____

_____

_____

Beyond the Classroom

Write down every penny you spend for the next two weeks on everything – from a pack of gum to a tank of gas to groceries and videos.

Go over your two-week record. Is there a pattern to your spending habits?

Think ahead to the future and earning "big bucks" in your job or profession. Will you have enough then? Can you put money in a savings account for the future? Are there habits you could change now?

_____

_____

_____

_____

_____

_____

_____

_____

_____

_____

_____

_____

_____

_____

_____

Section 10: Personal Health

How would you rate your health?

Some Information

The rules don't change: Get enough sleep
Eat at least five servings of fruits and vegetables a day
Exercise moderately to vigorously at least three times a week
Cut stress
Wear your seatbelt

The "don'ts" don't change: Don't overeat
Don't drink too much alcohol, abuse drugs or self-medicate
Don't gamble what you don't have
Don't smoke
Don't worry

Try some of these health-management tips:

- Walk the stairs in a building instead of taking the elevator.

- Look both ways when you cross the street.

- Eat breakfast. "Break the fast" of the night's sleep. Eat four or five smaller meals a day instead of one or two big meals. Eat fewer snacks and packaged foods.

- Make your bed a wonderful place to go.

- Get enough sleep. There's evidence linking the 1989 Exxon Valdez disaster and the Three Mile Island nuclear power meltdown to human error caused by lack of sleep.

- Wash your hands frequently.

- Watch funny movies. Read the comics.

- Meditate, pray, or be quiet at least ten minutes a day.

- Make appointments with yourself to read, write, play the piano – whatever sparks your passion and creativity. Keep those appointments.

Ideas to write about

Are you happy with your body, your energy level, and general well being? Why? Why not? Is it worth your time and attention to be healthy?

_____

_____

_____

_____

_____

_____

_____

_____

_____

_____

_____

_____

_____

_____

_____

_____

Beyond the Classroom

If you're unhappy, sick or injured, you miss out – in the classroom and on the job. How will being healthy pay off in your life now and in the future?

_____

_____

_____

_____

_____

_____

_____

_____

_____

_____

_____

_____

_____

_____

_____

_____

Section 11: Lifelong Learning

Do you like learning something new?

Some Information

Humans adapt. They change what they can't adapt to.

They learn how to build a better mousetrap or invent a computer or write a new, gripping story of courage.

It's likely that since humans first noticed birds they have dreamed of flying. A hundred years ago the Wright Brothers did it. And life changed dramatically yet again.

The difference is that now change happens more quickly than it did a hundred years ago. There's more to know. Easier access to information sometimes means "information overload."

We must learn to "actively learn" and to "think critically" all of our lives and likely will need "to go to school" all of our lives – classes, conferences, training sessions – to keep up with the burst of new information.

_____

_____

_____

_____

_____

_____

_____

_____

_____

_____

Ideas to write about

What is learning? Why is learning sometimes hard? How can learning be exciting?

_____

_____

_____

_____

_____

_____

_____

_____

_____

_____

_____

_____

_____

_____

_____

_____

Beyond the Classroom

The workplace has an impact on education and education has an impact on the workplace.

If you know the field or profession you want to go into, how will education impact your field and vice versa?

How can you hone your basic learning skills in order to keep yourself educated all your life?

_____

_____

_____

_____

_____

_____

_____

_____

_____

_____

_____

_____

_____

_____

Section 12: Creating The Life You Want

Do you think self-esteem is important to your success?

Some Information

- "Until you value yourself, you won't value your time. Until you value your time, you will not do anything with it." M. Scott Peck

- "It was when I found out that I could make mistakes that I knew I was on to something." Ornette Coleman

- "The most incomprehensible thing about the universe is that it is comprehensible." Albert Einstein

    Each human being is unique – and comprehensible.

    "Know thyself," the great sages have said.

The great sages also have said: "You can't change the world. You can only change yourself." Sounds simple. But it means knowing ourselves – our strengths and shortcomings. The goal is to feel good about our place in the world, then do good.

- "Be the change you wish to see in the world." Gandhi

    Your life is your life.

_____

_____

_____

_____

_____

_____

_____

Ideas to write about

Do you like yourself? Are you confident? Do you have others in your life that supports you?
Who have been your role models in your life? Who are the people you want in your life? Why?

_____

_____

_____

_____

_____

_____

_____

_____

_____

_____

_____

_____

_____

_____

_____

_____

Beyond the Classroom

Write down what you know.
Write down what you've accomplished.
List everything you're good at.

What more will you want to know two years from now? Five? Ten?
What will you have accomplished between now and two years from now? Five? Ten?
What else will you want to be good at in two years? Five? Ten?

How will you get from here to there?

_____

_____

_____

_____

_____

_____

_____

_____

_____

_____

_____

_____

_____

_____